Pocket Pal

Magic Tricks

Illustrator: Glen Singleton
Cover illustrator: Rob Kiely
Project editor: Katie Hewat
Designer: Diana Vlad

Published in 2009 by Hinkler Books Pty Ltd
45–55 Fairchild Street
Heatherton VIC 3202 Australia
www.hinklerbooks.com

ISBN: 978 1 7418 2118 5
Printed and bound in China

Contents

Introduction

So, you'd like to do magic tricks? Why?

If your answer is you'd like to perform in front of audiences at home or school, or even at parties or community festivals, read on, and we'll give you some great tips to create a captivating magic show.

If you just like the idea of learning some magic tricks to do in front of your family and close friends, that's fine, too. Either way, this is the book for you, because there are so many tricks contained in these pages, you will be able to keep everyone entertained for months!

Magic features in the myths and legends of cultures throughout the world. You may have heard of Merlin the Magician who, it was said, trained King Arthur to become

King of England more than 1,500 years ago. It was only Arthur who could pull the magic sword, Excalibur, from the rock in which Merlin had sunk it, and so he became king.

Although most of us can't explain how a microchip powers a computer or remember the principles of electricity once our science lesson is over, we readily accept what these and other marvels of technology can do for us. But who hasn't looked on in awe as a smiling magician makes a coin disappear or appear, seemingly at will? We love mysteries, and that's the appeal of magic.

Therefore, the first rule a magician must learn is: Never, ever tell anyone how to do a trick. It doesn't matter if the person is your best friend.

DO NOT TELL HOW A TRICK IS DONE!

Getting Started

There are a few rules to remember when performing magic tricks:

1   Never tell anyone how a trick is done. I know we've said this before, but it's the most important rule. DO NOT TELL!

2   Practise each trick in your repertoire until you know it perfectly and can do it over and over without a mistake.

3   Keep your audience directly in front of you. Don't let people sit beside or behind you.

4   Don't repeat a trick in front of the same audience. It may be flattering to be asked to do so, but the members of your audience are really only trying to see how the trick's done!

5   As a general rule, don't tell your audience what you are going to do. It's better to let anticipation and suspense build as you perform your trick. You can, however, talk to your audience. Talking, or patter, will help distract them, so they will not see what you are really doing!

6   Use expressions and gestures to enhance your act. For example, you can frown to show you are concentrating hard; or stand still without speaking to gain your audience's attention; or you might like to use sweeping arm gestures when you are calling upon your 'magical powers' or trying to distract your audience.

7   Make sure all your props are in perfect working order and look good – no scruffy wands or hats.

8   Once you have learned a trick and can perform it, you may choose to alter it. This can be fun!

9   Practise and perfect the story or patter you tell while performing each trick – it's what makes you different from another person who performs the same trick.

10   Perform against a dark background under a good light.

Putting on a Magic Show

Begin by learning simple tricks that interest you and require only a few props. You will find these tricks are the easiest to perform. As you become more confident, you can learn longer, more difficult tricks.

Then it will be time to plan your act!

Every well-planned act has a beginning, a middle and an end. When planning your act, remember to place shorter tricks between longer ones, as this will help to hold your audience's interest. Think about how long you want your show to be. When you are starting out, a good show is often a short show! Maybe you only want your show to last 10–15 minutes – that's still a

lot of talking and a lot of tricks when you
are new to magic!

Preparation

Apart from the obvious – learning your
tricks so you are really confident performing
them – you need to have the props for every
trick you will perform. It is a good idea to
cover a table with a cloth and put the props
on top of the cloth until they are needed.
Make sure your props look good!

Plan what you are going to wear. Dressing
up as a magician, even if you don't rely on
your costume for props, is a way of really
making you feel the part. You may need to
wear something special for certain tricks.

Also, if you have decided to weave a
special story or line of patter throughout
the show, practise this as much as your
tricks. You need to be confident with
everything!

Performing

When you are in front of your audience, act confident. Look excited about the magic tricks you are performing. Take your bows and enjoy the applause – that's one of the reasons you are there.

Speak as clearly as you can – if you mumble, your audience won't be able to follow what you are saying and may miss crucial pieces of information.

Always involve your audience by asking for volunteers and don't worry if something goes wrong. Either repeat it, if appropriate, or begin the next trick.

Plan your show so your best trick is performed last and you go out on a cheer!

Finally, have fun!

Quick Tricks and Simple Illusions

Begin your show with a couple of these quick and simple illusions. They will leave your audience wanting more!

Mind Reading

Tricks that involve mind reading and
numbers are always fascinating. Here's an
easy and effective one to include in your
show.

1 Ask a friend to write down a number. It
can be any number (it doesn't matter how
many digits) provided the digits do not
decrease in value. Your friend should not
show you the number until the end of the
trick.

2 Ask your friend to
multiply the number
she wrote down by
10. (Let's pretend
your friend chose the number 15689.)

15689
X 10
156890

16

3 Ask your friend to subtract the first number from the second number.

$$\begin{array}{r} 156890 \\ -\ 15689 \\ \hline 41201 \end{array}$$

4 Ask your friend to add 9 to the answer.

$$\begin{array}{r} 141201 \\ +\ 9 \\ \hline 141210 \end{array}$$

5 Ask your friend to cross out any number except a zero and tell you what the remaining digits are. In our example, the second 1 is crossed out and the remaining numbers are 1, 4, 2, 1 and 0.

6   You add these remaining digits in your head – they come to 8 – and then subtract the total from 9 to find out what number was crossed out.

7   Tell your friend the number she crossed out was 1! Mind reading wins again!

Arrow-cadabra

★ You need: a pencil. a sheet of paper. a glass (straight-sided). a jug of water. a table

This magic trick is a great one to do before a small audience.

1 Fold the sheet of paper in half and draw an arrow in the middle of one side.

2 Stand the folded sheet on a table with the arrow facing the audience. Place the empty glass in front of it. Now challenge a member of the audience to turn the arrow around without touching the paper or the glass.

19

3 Of course, he can't do it unless, unhappily, he has seen the trick done before! You do it by producing the jug of water (which until now has been out of sight) and filling the glass with water.

4 Presto! The arrow turns to face the opposite way!

Did you Know?

Magicians are often very theatrical performers, more so than actors! Magicians use grand gestures to distract audiences from what is really happening during a show!

Magic Paper Rings

This quick little illusion will have your audience believing you can do anything!

1 Hold the paper strip and twist it once.

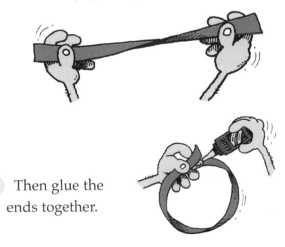

2 Then glue the ends together.

21

3 Cut around the centre of the ring carefully. What's the result? Two rings? No, it's one big ring if you've cut correctly.

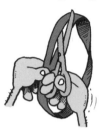 

4 Now to take this a little further, cut around the centre again. Do you think you'll get a really big ring this time? No! This time there are two rings!

Vanishing Pencil

★ **You need:** a coin. a blunt pencil

Tell your audience you can make a coin disappear – but it seems you need more practice!

1 Stand with your left side towards your audience if you are right-handed or your right side towards them if you are left-handed. Put the coin in the hand closest to the audience and hold it up, explaining that it will disappear once you tap it sharply three times with your pencil.

2 Hold the end of the pencil with the fingers of your other hand and bring it up into the air until it is level with your ear.

3 Bring the pencil down and tap the coin sharply with it while exclaiming a really loudly 'One!'.

4 Do this again, bringing the pencil up to exactly the same height and down again, tapping the coin and saying 'Two!'.

5 Without missing a beat, bring the pencil up one more time, this time sliding it easily and quickly behind your ear. Bring your now-empty hand down, saying 'Three!', and look really surprised to discover the pencil has vanished.

6 Turn away from the audience, without showing the pencil if possible, and mutter something about having to go and practise the trick more.

7 Remember – to succeed with this trick you need to keep the same 'beat' going when counting. Don't pause between any of the taps of the coin, especially not before the third tap!

Hey... I'm not a happy Pharoah.../ What happened to the Vanishing Pyramid Trick and turning a camel into a palm tree?

Did you know?
The first record of performing magicians is in the Westcar Papyrus in the State Museum of Berlin, Germany. It contains documented proof that magicians performed for the Pharaohs of ancient Egypt about 4500 years ago.

The Coin Really Disappears This Time

★ You need: a coin, a pencil, a table

This trick follows on beautifully from the previous one, but can be a stand-alone trick if you prefer.

1   Begin by sitting at a table with your side to the audience. If your dominant hand (that is the hand you do most things with) is your right hand, sit with your left hand towards the audience, and vice versa if you are left-handed.

2 Repeat the Vanishing Pencil trick (but stay seated). When you count 'Three!', act surprised the pencil  has vanished and look questioningly at the audience. At first they'll be surprised, but then you should let them see the pencil stuck behind your ear, and they'll begin laughing. You should laugh, too.

3 Reach up with your dominant hand to remove the pencil. Now here's the clever bit: while you are removing the pencil  with one hand (and hopefully the whole audience is watching you do that), the hand holding the coin quickly tips it into your lap.

27

4   As the coin leaves your hand, close your hand into a fist (you want the audience to think you are still holding the coin).

5   Say something along the lines of: 'Well, I tricked you there, but now let me really make the coin disappear'. Lift the pencil and tap your closed fist with it, then open your hand to show the coin has gone!

Pocket Puzzler

★ You need: a deck of cards.
a calculator. a piece of paper.
a pencil

Using your magical powers, you are able
to name the card hidden in an assistant's
pocket.

1 Ask a volunteer
to come forward
and write down
any four-digit
number on a piece
of paper, without
letting you see any
of the numbers.

The only condition is the four numbers
must be different. (In our example, we'll
use the number 7539.)

2   Ask him to add the four numbers together and write down the total. Now give him the calculator and ask him to subtract the total from the original number.

$$7+5+3+9=24$$

$$\begin{array}{r} 7539 \\ -24 \\ \hline 7515 \end{array}$$

3   Hand the volunteer a deck of cards and ask him to secretly remove four cards that have the same numbers as the four digits in his answer. (An ace = 1 and a king = 0.) Each card must be a different suit.

4   Ask your volunteer to put one card (that isn't a king) in his pocket, or out of sight, and hand you the

30

other three
cards. In our
example, the
volunteer puts
the five of clubs
in his pocket.

5 Now you must mentally add the values
of the three cards. If the answer has more
than one digit, add those digits until there
is only one digit. (For example, 13 becomes
$1 + 3 = 4$).

6 Mentally subtract this number from 9, and
the value of the card in your volunteer's
pocket will
appear, as if by
magic! It's a 5 and,
because you are
holding cards
that are hearts,

$7 + 1 + 5 = 13$
$1 + 3 = 4$
$9 - 4 = 5$

spades and diamonds, the card must be
the 5 of clubs!

7 The only exception to this clever little
trick is when you mentally subtract the
value of the cards from 9 and the answer is
0 – the missing card isn't a king, it's a 9.

33

Diabolically Clever
Card Tricks

Many young magicians include card tricks in their magic shows. This is a good idea. Nearly every household has a deck or two of cards lying about. so no extra money needs to be spent on props. and there are many simple card tricks you can learn that look great when performed!

Who's Lying

Card tricks are a magician's stock-in-trade. Everyone expects you to be able to flip, shuffle, twist and 'read' cards telepathically – so let's get on with it!

1   Before your audience arrives, shuffle the deck of cards. Make sure you know which card is on the bottom.

2   Once your audience is seated, fan out the deck of cards on the table in front of you and ask a volunteer to choose one card. She is not to show or tell you its identity.

3 While the volunteer looks at the card, you
should close the fan of cards, straighten the
deck and place it on the table, face down.
Ask the volunteer to cut the deck into two
equal piles and put her card on the pile she
cut from the top of the deck.

4 Now ask your volunteer to place the other
half of the deck on top of this. This should
mean the card you memorised, which was
at the bottom of the
pile a minute ago,
is now on top of
the selected card.

5 Now is the time for some good magician's patter. Explain to the audience the deck of cards is special – it can detect lies!

6 Explain to your volunteer that you are going to turn each card over and ask her if this is the card she selected. She is to say 'no' every time, even when you turn over her selected card. The deck of cards will 'tell' you when she is lying. Obviously you are looking for the card you memorised – the card after it will be the selected card.

7 When you turn over the selected card and your volunteer says 'No', yell 'Liar!' loudly and watch her reaction!

Find the Queen

★ You need: five playing cards
(four black cards and one red
queen). glue. a peg

This trick is really an optical illusion. All
your volunteer has to do is find the queen
– but it's harder to do than it seems.

1 Before facing your audience you need
to prepare the cards. Arrange them in an
overlapping line – first, three black cards,
then the red queen, then the fourth black
card. Now glue them in place and leave
them to dry overnight.

2 Once your audience arrives, show them
the strip of cards, pointing out the red
queen. Ask a volunteer to remember where
it is.

3 After handing the volunteer the peg, turn the cards around so the backs of the cards face the audience. Ask your volunteer to clip the peg onto the queen.

4 Once he has clipped the peg onto a card, turn the strip of cards around. Your volunteer will be astonished to see his guess wasn't right because this looks so easy to do! More than likely (and you can test this yourself), the card that was pegged was the last card.

The Chosen Card

★ You need: a deck of cards.
a table

This trick requires some preparation, but when it's done properly, it's a real winner!

1 Separate the cards by colour. Make a pile of red cards and a pile of black cards. Put one pile on top of the other, so you now have a deck of cards separated into two coloured halves. Now it's time to bring on the audience!

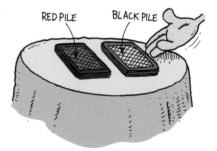

RED PILE   BLACK PILE

2 Pick up the cards and hold the deck face down in your left palm if you are right-handed and in your right palm if you are left-handed. With your other hand, begin to flick the cards with your thumb at the end nearest you. This way, you are the only one who can see the faces of the cards. Flick upward from the bottom of the deck. You don't have to actually see the numbers and suits, you want to see when the colours change. While you are doing this, explain to the audience that you are going to cut the deck into two equal piles.

3 Once the colour changes, you stop and cut the deck. Only you know that you have cut the deck into two equal piles of different-coloured cards – your audience thinks you have just cut the cards into two roughly equal piles, especially when you say: 'I think the piles look the same'.

4 Ask for a volunteer.

5 Take one pile (let's say the red one) and spread the cards face down in your hands and ask the volunteer to take a card and remember it. He can even show it to the rest of the audience if he wants to.

6 While he is doing that, put down those cards and pick up the other pile (in this case, the black one). Spread this one out in the same way and tell the volunteer to place the selected card into this half of the deck.

7   Put the cards together again to make one
    deck and ask the volunteer if he would like
    to cut the deck. He can do this as many
    times as he likes. (Because your volunteer
    placed a red card into the black half of the
    deck, it doesn't matter how many times
    the cards are cut. When you begin to look
    through the cards, you will see clusters of
    same-coloured cards together. When you
    see one red card in a cluster of black cards,
    you will know this is the chosen card.)
    However, do not let your volunteer shuffle
    the cards – if he does, then you will not be
    able to find the chosen card!

8   It is possible that the chosen card will end
    up on the top or the bottom of the deck. If
    you cannot see a single red card in a black
    cluster, then check the top or bottom card.
    If you find a red card next to some black
    ones, it is the chosen card.

The Talking Cards

★ You need: a deck of cards with no jokers, a table

You can find any card in a deck by listening to your 'talking' cards . . .

1 Explain to your audience that you have special powers that enable you to hear 'talking' cards – even though they won't be able to hear anything!

2 Ask a volunteer to deal out the cards face up on the table. He must deal them out in a single row until you say 'Stop'. You should mentally count the number of cards being dealt, taking note of the seventh card. When your volunteer reaches 26, tell him to stop and say something like: 'That should be enough cards to choose from'.

3 Now tell the audience you'll select a card
   at random from those on the table. Pretend
   to consider the cards, then point to the
   seventh card. Ask your volunteer to tell
   the audience the name of the selected card.
   Explain to your audience that you will be
   able to find the selected card again with the
   help of your 'talking' cards.

4 Pick up the cards in the same order they
   were dealt, stacking the second card on top
   of the first and so on. Put the stack of cards
   face down on the table and put the rest of
   the deck face down on top.

5 Slowly deal out the cards, so that they
   lie face up in a column. Tell the audience
   the cards are 'talking' to you. Note the
   number of the first card. Continue to deal
   and silently count from that number until
   you reach 10. For example, if the first card
   is a 4, the next card becomes 5, then 6, 7, 8,

9 and 10 – no matter what the numbers on the cards actually are.

6 Once you reach number 10, start another column – all the while pretending the cards are 'talking' to you. If the first card you turn over in a column is a 10 or a face card, such as a king or queen, it counts as 10, and you must begin the next column. Aces count as 1.

7 Make three columns and then stop. Stare at the cards and while the audience thinks you are 'listening' to them, mentally add up the three cards at the tops of the columns. Perhaps these are 10, 3 and 2, which would make 15. This number is the key to finding the selected card!

8 Now tell the audience the cards have told you the location of the selected card. Tell the volunteer to deal off the same number of

cards as your total – in our example, that is 15. The fifteenth card will be your selected card! The volunteer and audience will be amazed!

9 Try this trick a few times on your own or for your parents and see how easy it is!

Choices

In this trick, you ask a volunteer to deal you a card seemingly at random – but, in fact, you already know the card's identity!

1   Before your show, memorise the tenth card from the top of a deck of cards.

2   Begin the trick by giving a volunteer the deck of cards. Ask her to think of a number between 10 and 20, then ask her to deal that number of cards face down into a stack on the table. The rest of the deck can be put aside.

3   Now your volunteer needs to add together the two digits that make up the number she selected. If she selected the

number 14, for example, she would add 1 and 4 to get 5. She then deals that number of cards, 5, from the stack and looks at the fifth card without telling anyone what it is. This card will be the card you memorised before the trick – the original tenth card.

4 Pretend to read the volunteer's mind. Perhaps you'd like to heighten the drama by drawing the card on a piece of paper. Or you could ask the volunteer to return the card to the deck and shuffle the cards. She hands the deck to you and you 'select' the card by 'reading her fingerprints'!

5 However you do it, you'll be right every time!

52

Topsy-turvy

Make a magician out of a volunteer with this trick. Your volunteer will pick a card, place it back in the deck, wave a magic wand – and presto! – the card will have magically turned over in the deck!

1 Before the audience arrives, turn over the bottom card in the deck so the deck looks the same from both ends.

2 From your audience, select a volunteer. Then fan out the cards face down in your hands, taking care not to show the reversed card on the bottom of the deck. Ask your volunteer to select a card and show it to the audience, but not to you.

3   As the volunteer is showing the card to the audience, you should close the deck in the palm of one hand and secretly turn it over so that the reversed bottom card is now on top of the deck. You need to practise this movement to make it so smooth that no one will notice you doing it.

4   Ask your volunteer to place the card face down anywhere she likes in the deck that you are still holding. What she's done, of course, is place the selected card backward in the deck of cards.

5   Now tell the volunteer she is going to perform the magic trick with the help of your magic wand (if you have one) or some magic words that you will tell her. Turn over the hand holding the deck, so it is now palm down, and put the deck of cards flat on the table. Now the deck is right-side up again with the reversed card

on the bottom of the deck. The selected
card is also reversed.

6 Once your volunteer has woven her magic
spell over the cards, you can fan out the
cards on the table or move them from hand
to hand until you come to the selected
card, which, of course, will be reversed face
up within the deck. Show the audience the
card. Congratulate your new assistant and
take the applause with her!

Create an Image

This trick relies on a good setup!

1 Before your audience arrives, glue a small
make-up mirror on the back of the box of
cards. This may need
to dry overnight. Keep
the deck of cards in
the box, with the flap
closed.

2 To begin your
performance, hold the
box of cards in one
hand with the mirror facing you. Remove
the deck of cards with the other hand and

fan out the cards face down on the table. Keep hold of the box.

3 Ask someone in the audience to choose a card, look at it, memorise it, and then hand it to you. The card face must be turned away from you. (You are still holding the box and may need to mention this in the patter you devise for the trick.)

4   Take the card, making sure the face is still turned towards the audience and your volunteer, and say something like: 'I need the help of the magic box to sense the suit and number of the card'. Then move the card behind the box so it is possible for you to glimpse the card in the mirror.

5   Keep the patter going by asking your volunteer to concentrate on the card he chose and to send a mental image of it to you. Place the box on the table (once

you know what the card is!), ensuring the mirror can't be seen, and put the card on top of the box so it will release its magic powers. Then proudly tell the audience what card the volunteer chose!

6 Don't do this trick more than once before the same audience, as it is too easy for someone to ask why you are holding on to the box. Someone may even see the mirror!

Arise Card

★ You need: a deck of cards

Make any card you name rise out of the deck.

1. Ask a volunteer to shuffle the deck of cards.

2. When the deck is handed back to you, straighten it, taking note of which card is face down on top. Perhaps it is the ten of diamonds.

3. Hold the deck vertically in one hand (left if you are right-handed and right if you are left-handed), so the cards are facing the audience.

4. Place your other hand behind the deck and rest your forefinger or index finger on

60

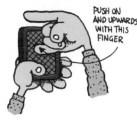

PUSH ON AND UPWARDS WITH THIS FINGER

top of the deck. Now extend your little finger (or ring finger if it is easier) until it touches the back of the top card (the ten of diamonds).

5 Now all you need to do is name the card and ask it to rise for you! 'Ten of diamonds . . . arise now from your slumber!' While you are saying this, push upward on the top card with your little or ring finger. Do it slowly, making sure your forefinger or index finger is rising as you speak. From where the audience is sitting it will look as if your forefinger or index

finger is encouraging the rising card to rise, and it will also look as if the card is coming from the middle of the deck. Easy, but effective!

What's Gone?

You'll need to concentrate while performing this trick. But do it well, and you'll earn yourself a reputation as a good magician.

1 Hand one person in the audience nine cards in any suit – ace through to 9.

2 Ask your assistant to shuffle the cards. While he or she is shuffling, you should take a seat with your back to the table.

3 Tell your assistant to deal the cards into three rows with three cards in each.

4 Now ask your assistant to remove one card, show it to the audience, then put the card in her pocket.

5 The assistant now adds up the cards in the columns, ignoring the space where the removed card once was. In our example, the answers are 13, 15 and 10.

6 Your assistant now adds up the digits in the answers. In our example, that would be 1 + 3 + 1 + 5 + 1 + 0 = 11. Your assistant tells you the total, which in this case is 11. Without pausing or turning around to look

at the cards or the audience, you press your fingers to your head and say: 'You removed the 7'.

7   You have deduced this answer on a simple mathematical basis. You always subtract the number given to you from the number 9, or a multiple of 9. For example, we know that 11 cannot be subtracted from 9, so for any number greater than 8 you subtract it from 18. Therefore, $18 - 11 = 7$ – presto! You're right! (Should the number be greater than 17, simply subtract it from 27.)

Card Telepathy

If you practise and perfect this illusion, it looks really impressive, but you do need to be able to memorise a couple of cards at a time. This is a great trick to begin a show . . . it makes you look so good!

1   First ask a person from your audience to shuffle the deck and then hand it back to you. Explain to your audience that you will use telepathy to 'read' the card that is at the front of the deck facing them.

2   Now for the secret to your success. There are two things you do – first, you put the deck behind your back and, making sure

the audience doesn't see you, you take the front card and move it to the back of the deck, facing in the reverse direction.

3 The next thing you do is have a 'dummy' run, by saying to everyone: 'Now this is what we're going to do!' Explain in more detail as you hold up the deck of cards with the reversed card facing the audience. Don't guess the card this time. Instead you memorise the card facing you.

4 Now, begin. Put the deck behind your back and move the card you memorised to the other side of the deck, facing in the reverse direction (as in step 2). Hold up the deck with the reversed card facing the audience and correctly name the card facing them. Each time you hold the deck up to the audience, facing you is the next card you will show them and the next

card you will 'guess' correctly. You must
memorise it!

5   For this trick to work well, you need to
string the audience along and not guess the
card immediately. Pretend to be reading
their minds as they concentrate on the card
they can see. Say things like: 'I feel it's a
card with red vibrations' or 'It's one of the
lower-numbered cards in hearts'. Press the
fingers of your free hand to your forehead
while 'thinking'.

6 Around three or four cards into the trick say: 'This will be the last card, because concentrating this hard always gives me a headache'.

It's Time

⭐ You need: a deck of cards.
a watch

When you begin this trick, you might like
to make references to Alice in Wonderland
and the White Rabbit, who was always
looking at his watch and saying, 'I'm late,
I'm late, for a very important date'. You
will use your watch in this trick.

1   Ask four volunteers to choose a card each.
All the volunteers should look at all the
cards. You should not look at any of them.

2   The volunteers then discuss secretly
which of the four cards they prefer while
you divide the rest of the cards into
two equal face-down piles.

3 Ask the volunteers to hand you the chosen card. Do not look at it. Ask the volunteers which pile they want their chosen card to be placed upon. Place it there, then place the other three cards on the other pile.

4 Once this is done, you pick up the pile with the three cards on top and place it on top of the other pile, so the single chosen card is now in the middle of the deck.

SINGLE CARD ON TOP

PILE WITH 3 CARDS ON TOP

5 The reference to the time is brought in now. You look at your watch and tell everyone it's 17 minutes past 11, for

example. Ask a volunteer to add these numbers together – to get a total of 28 – then deal out the cards to 'magically' reveal the chosen card is in fact the twenty-eighth down in the deck!

6 Of course, you can only use this trick when the time will add up to 28: at 12:16, 1:27, 2:26, 3:25 and so on.

Cards That Spell

★ You need: a deck of cards.
a table

Prove to your audience that cards can
spell their own numbers! This trick –
simple, but very effective – relies on
the magician remembering the correct
sequence when picking up the scattered
cards.

1   You'll need to create some patter
explaining that you've discovered cards
can actually spell and you think spades (or
whatever suit you choose) is the smartest
suit.

2   Once you've selected your suit, take all
13 cards from the suit out of the deck.
While doing this, place the 13 cards face
up on a table in a random, scattered way.

If they are scattered fairly widely across the table it will seem less likely you are actually going to pick them up in a particular order. Put the rest of the deck aside.

3 Now pick up the spades in the following order: queen, 4, ace, 8, king, 2, 7, 5, 10, jack, 3, 6, 9. (Make sure the queen is at the top of the pack when it is face down, and the 9 is on the bottom.)

4 Now all you have to do is have fun and remember how to spell!

5 Begin by spelling out A-C-E. When you say 'A', put the first card at the bottom of the pile. When you say 'C', put the second card at the bottom of the pile. When you say 'E', reveal the third card to be, in fact, the ace. This card is put aside.

6 Next spell out T-W-O in the same way. Again, when you get to the third card, you will turn up the 2. Put it aside on top of the ace.

7 Continue in this way, spelling out T-H-R-E-E, F-O-U-R, F-I-V-E and so on, until the final card left is the king.

Always Red

★ You need: two decks of cards with different-coloured designs on the back (one design should be red). a piece of paper. a pen or pencil. a table

As a magician it's great to involve your audience. In this trick you write a prediction on a piece of paper and give it to an audience member. The prediction states: 'You will pick the only red card out of the six cards'. And that's what happens!

1 You need to pick out six cards for this trick. One must be the ace of spades or clubs from the deck with the red design on the back. One must be the 6 of hearts or diamonds from the other deck, and the other four cards can be any clubs or spades

75

from the same deck with values of 7 or greater.

2. Before your audience arrives, arrange the six chosen cards in the following order at the top of the deck (the one without the red design on the back): other, ace, 6, other, other, other.

3. Once your audience arrives, ask for a volunteer. As she stands with you at the table, write your prediction down and show her and the audience.

4 Next, deal the top six cards as follows:
face down, face up, face down, face up,
face down, face up.

RED BACK

SIX OF DIAMONDS

5 Now the volunteer gives you a number
between 1 and 6 – let's say she chooses
4. Remember you've predicted she will
choose a red card, so count from right to
left and you get to turn over the six of
hearts or diamonds.

If the volunteer chooses 1, you pick up
the ace and show the red-backed design. If
she chooses 2, count from left to right and

show the ace. For 3, count from left to right
to get to the 6 of hearts or diamonds. For
5, count from right to left to get to the ace,
and for 6, pick up the 6 of diamonds or
hearts straight away.

6   Don't do this trick again in the same show
    – it becomes too obvious you knew what
    cards were there!

Your Card Is ...

⭐ You need: a deck of cards

This is another simple but effective trick
to show you are a master or mistress of the
cards! Yet again, you will find the 'selected'
card hidden in the deck. Remember to deal
the cards the same way every time.

1   Deal out three piles with seven cards in
    each pile. Lay them out one, one, one, and
    two, two, two, rather than dealing one pile
    at a time. Put the remainder of the deck
    aside – it won't be needed.

2 Ask an audience member to pick a card from any pile and to remember it, but not tell anyone what it is. He should then put the card back in the same pile.

3 You now gather up the three piles of cards, making sure the pile with the selected card is between the other two piles, then deal them out again, into three groups of seven cards.

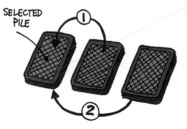

SELECTED PILE

4 Ask your volunteer to inspect each pile of cards and tell you which pile the selected card is now in.

5 Again, gather all the piles of cards, keeping the selected card's pile between the other two piles, and deal them out into three groups of seven.

6 The volunteer again finds his selected card and indicates to you which pile it is now in. You gather the piles up, again keeping the selected card's pile between the other two.

7 Spell out Y-O-U-R-C-A-R-D-I-S by removing a card for each letter – and the next card will be the selected card!

81

Into Thin Air

So you've dazzled the audience by finding the cards they've picked, but how about making cards disappear? That would be fun . . .

1 A little bit of preparation for this trick is necessary. Make sure the toothpick is as long as the width of a playing card – if it's too long, trim it. Now poke this toothpick into the hem of the handkerchief. You're ready for an audience!

2 Begin with a flourish by

spreading the deck of cards on the table.
Wave the handkerchief about and tell your
audience you'll pick a card from the deck
and make it vanish into thin air.

3 Lay the
handkerchief over
the cards so the edge
with the toothpick
is folded under the
handkerchief.

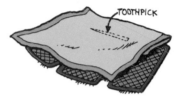

4 Pick up the edge of
the handkerchief that
contains the toothpick
by holding the
toothpick between your
thumb and index finger
– it looks as if you are
holding a card, right?

5 Say your favourite magic words,
   including something about making the card
   disappear. Throw the handkerchief into the
   air – the card appears to have vanished!

Cunning Coin
Conundrums

Coins are easy to find around the home, so
they are perfect for the budding magician to
use in tricks. Of course, there are trick coins –
double-headed and specialty – available at magic
shops, but for most of the following tricks any
coin will do!

Sleight of Hand

All magicians learn sleight of hand. Learn this trick well and you can perform it at any time in any place: a show, a party or even a restaurant!

1. Begin by placing the coin firmly between the first knuckles of the index and middle fingers of one hand. The coin should be hidden, so that when you present your open hand (palm out) to the audience, they can't see a thing.

From the other side... Can't see the coin

2. Now we come to the part that you need to practise and practise. To produce the coin you turn your fingers in toward the

palm of your hand
and use your thumb
to flip the coin
upward.

Did you know?

By the 1800s, magic was
often performed in theatres
in many countries. At some
venues, magicians performed
regularly.

Spin That Coin

This is so simple, it's not really a trick. In fact, anyone can do it, but you're the one who has practised and practised to make sure it works every time!

1. Place the coin on the table and pick it up gently between the points of the pins.

2. Once you're sure it's secure, blow really gently on the coin, and it will begin to spin.

90

3 That's all there is to it! It's a great trick to open a small magic show. You only need to keep the coin spinning for a few seconds – or longer if you like – to ensure that the audience thinks you're a great magician!

The Coin Fold

Another easy but effective trick using just
one coin – especially suitable for a small
audience.

1   Place the coin in the
centre of the piece of
paper.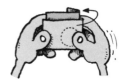

2   Fold the bottom edge
of the paper up and over
the coin, leaving a 6-mm
(25-in) gap between the
two edges of the paper.

3   Fold the right edge of the
paper back behind the coin.

92

4 Then fold the left edge of the paper back
   behind the coin.

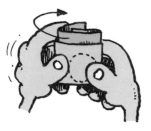

5 Make the final fold by bending the top
   flap of the paper back behind the coin. It
   seems as if the coin is completely wrapped,
   but in fact the top edge is still open.

6 You now turn the package around so the open edge allows the coin to slip into the palm of your hand, where it stays while you 'prove' the coin has disappeared by tearing up the paper package.

Now You See It.
Now You Don't!

Actually the saying needs to be reversed for this disappearing and reappearing coin. Read on!

1　Before the show begins, make a magic cone from the single sheet of coloured paper. Secure it with glue and add stars and glitter to make it look magical.

95

2　Next, cut a circle from one of the other sheets of paper using the glass as your guide and glue it to the rim of the glass. This will cover the coin and will not be seen, as it will be resting on a sheet of same-coloured paper. Put the magic cone, glass and coin on the remaining sheet of paper. (The glass should be upside down.) Now you're ready for your audience.

3　Tell your audience the cone is endowed with magic powers and can make things disappear. You will make the coin disappear.

4 Cover the glass with the cone and place both over the coin. Tap the cone with a wand or simply wave your hands while saying magic words, such as 'Abracadabra!'

5 Lift up the cone to show the glass, but no coin – it has been magically spirited away.

6 Of course, the coin is really still on the table, but the paper on the rim of the glass is covering the coin. Therefore, it's easy for you to be a really clever magician and restore the coin to the table by reversing the process.

Place the cone over the glass again, use a few simple magic words and a flourish of hands, and pick up the cone and the glass. There it is – the coin has reappeared!

Did you Know?

Popular magicians took their travelling shows around the world. Early in the twentieth century, one American magician had his Wonder Show of the Universe touring the world. He was America's top performer for 30 years.

The Chemical Coin

You'll also need some good patter. It's
best to perform this intriguing trick before
a small audience.

1   Your story should begin as soon as the
audience arrives. Talk excitedly about
what you've just read on the Internet – that
chemicals in the human body can break
down the metals that make up a coin. In
fact, coins can just disappear!

2   Show the coin to your audience and sit
down at your table resting your chin on
your right hand. Begin rubbing the coin
held in your left hand against your right
forearm, making sure no one can actually
see the coin as you do this.

3 While you are rubbing the coin on your
   arm, continue telling the fantastic story
   you began your show with. Now the coin
   should slip out of your left hand and drop
   on to the table. Continue with the story
   and make sure you are looking at your
   audience.

4 Pick up the dropped coin in your right hand and pretend to pass it back into your left hand, but actually keep it in your right hand.

5 Prop up your chin again in your right hand and pretend to rub the coin on your forearm as before. This movement must be done really masterfully and you must continue telling your story while this happens.

6 Keep on rubbing for a little longer, then suddenly look a little concerned. Continue to rub – maybe even a bit harder – and then slowly stop the

rubbing, lifting your left-hand fingers one at a time.

At the same time, you carefully drop the coin into your shirt collar. Then, with a flourish, show your audience the coin has disappeared, just as you predicted!

The Coin Tells

You'll be amazed at how simple this trick is – don't forget to learn some good patter to ensure your audience is really convinced it's magic!

1 Place the four coins on the table while talking about telepathy. Ask an audience member to choose a coin while your back is turned. Tell her to hold it tightly and concentrate hard so you can pick up the vibes from her mind!

2 Concentrate silently for a few moments, pretending you are trying to pick up thought waves – but what you're really doing is slowly counting to 30.

3 When you reach 30, say dispiritedly that you aren't receiving any thoughts from her and accuse her of not concentrating hard enough. Whatever she says, ask for the coin to be put back on the table with

the others while you're still not looking,
and say that you'll get the coins to tell you
which one was selected.

4 Turn around and pick up each coin in
turn and hold it up to your ear to 'hear' it
'talking' to you. What you're really doing
is feeling each coin, because the one that
has been held by your volunteer will be
much warmer than the others.

5 Once you find the warmest coin, show it to the audience and wait for the applause!

Snatch!

Again, a simple coin trick that makes the magician look very, very clever! The idea is to put a coin in the palm of your hand and challenge a volunteer to snatch it from you before you can close your hand. Your volunteer can't do it, but when you switch places, you get the coin on your first try.

1   Put the coin on your palm and keep it flat. Have your volunteer hold his hand above yours.

2   Your volunteer now tries to grab the coin before you close your hand – be as quick as you can. Your volunteer will fail every time.

3   Now swap.

4   How do you do it? Place your fingers and
    thumb together, without touching, and
    make sure these fingers are pointing down
    toward the coin.

5   Quickly move your hand down, gently
    striking the palm of your volunteer's hand
    with your fingertips. This action means
    the volunteer's hand will be pushed
    downward a little, and the coin will jump
    up into your waiting fingers. Try it! It
    works!

Classic Conjuring

Every magician needs to spend some time
perfecting a few classic magic tricks. Don't worry
if some of the tricks seem old-fashioned or so
well-known you think everyone will know how
they're done: it's what you say and how you
perform them that your friends will love. You'll
probably think of a new way to do one or more
of them anyway. That's OK – magic doesn't stay
the same.

Long Arm

Perhaps not a classic trick, but a classic effect. People love seeing a magician do something they don't think they can do themselves.

1 You'll need to practise this trick over and over again – try doing it in front of a mirror so you can see the effect you are trying to create. You do need to wear a jacket or a coat while performing (and practising) this trick.

2 First, stand still and bend your arm so your left hand and wrist are level with your waist.

3 Now, with the other hand, pinch the loose skin on the back of your left hand near the knuckle of the middle finger.

4 Shake this skin loose a little. As you do, it appears you're actually stretching your arm by tugging it out of its sleeve to an abnormal length. That's all there is to this trick, but it's so effective when done really well and with a great story. For example, you could make up a tale about a trip to Longreach (a real place!).

PRESS SLEEVE AGAINST YOU HERE

5   Once you've pulled out the really long arm, you can tap your arm back inside the jacket sleeve as part of the story.

6   The effect is created by hugging the jacket or coat sleeve tightly to your body as you move your arm a normal length. Don't let the audience see your elbow just above the hem of the sleeve or you'll give the trick away!

Where's My Thumb?

This trick takes much longer to read about than to do! But you'll need to practise for several weeks before you'll be ready to perform it. You want your audience to believe the tip of your left thumb is being magically removed – without any blood! – from your hand.

1　How do you do this? Begin by holding your left hand in front of you, at about waist height. The palm of your hand faces you; your fingers are flat and pointing to the right. Make sure your thumb is parallel to your index finger.

113

2 Pretend to pull the tip off your left thumb with your right thumb and index finger. Make a big deal of this with lots of grunts and groans and twisted facial expressions! Of course you can't do it, can you?

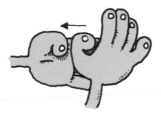

3 Well maybe you can! Try again, and this time, as you place your right index finger over the left thumb joint, bend the top of your left thumb down and put your right thumb so it looks as if it has replaced it.

4 Well, if you thought that was difficult, wait until you try this part! Tuck the other fingers of the right hand away so the audience can

clearly see your right thumb tip – which, of course, now looks as if it is your left thumb tip! Got it? Good!

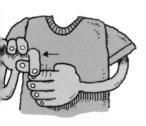

5 To complete the illusion, keep your left hand still and slowly slide the right thumb along the top of your left index finger. Then slowly slide it back to the original spot.

6 When your thumbs touch, show your hands with thumbs intact to your audience! Take a bow!

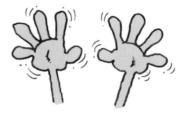

Pass-through Hand

This trick will entertain everyone when you perform it smoothly and with lots of great acting!

1 Make a fist with your left hand and hold the coin above it in your right hand.

2 Tell your audience that you intend to push the coin right through your hand. Begin pushing the coin down between the fingers of your left hand.

COIN PUSHED IN BETWEEN FINGERS

3   As it goes, it will slide out of sight behind your fingers, so you can proudly announce that it's 'gone through' your hand.

4   You open your fist, but there is no coin, so you have to pretend you think it's stuck halfway! Ask your audience where they think it is – there will nearly always be people who think they know!

5   Try again and this time add the tricky bit. As you turn your left hand back over into a fist, your thumb nearly touches the fingers holding the coin. Just as this happens, let the coin slip down from your fingers into your left hand at the same time as you make it into a fist again.

6   Because you've practised and practised, it all goes smoothly. The audience will tell you they think

the coin is still hidden by your fingers
somehow. Say you'll push harder this time,
and then slowly turn your fist and open it
up to reveal the coin!

The Classic Scarf Trick

★ You need: a long silky scarf.
a high-necked top

Most of the classic tricks are very simple, just like this one. The real trick for a magician – young or old – is to be smooth and professional!

1 Prepare for this trick by tucking the silky scarf into the neck of your high-necked top at the front and sides only.

2 In front of your audience, hold the ends of the scarf securely and pull both ends forward on the count of

three, or perhaps while chanting 'Sim Sala Bim!'

3 To complete the illusion, pull the scarf forward in one quick motion so it appears to pass straight through your neck! Wait for the applause!

How Eggstraordinary!

⭐ **You need:** an egg. a pencil.
a silk hankie. a teaspoon.
an egg cup (optional)

Done well, with lots of clever patter, this trick will make your audience believe you can pull a hankie out of an egg.

1 First, carefully prepare the egg. Make a hole in the side of an uncooked egg. Gently drain the contents of the egg and save them to eat later. Wash the shell inside and let it sit and dry naturally. Once the shell has dried, carefully poke your silk hankie into the hole with a pencil.

2 Now you need to convince your audience you have lost your hankie, but you're going to eat an egg instead. Of course, they will think it's a boiled egg, so when you hold it up in the air for the audience to see – keeping the hole toward you – you could pretend it's hot.

 3 Now, pop the egg back on the table and tap it gently with your spoon, then gasp and say something like: 'How eggstraordinary! You'll never guess where I've found my hankie'.

4 Break the egg apart excitedly, pull out the hankie and wave it in the air.

How Many Balls?

★ You need: three small
sponge balls

To do this trick, you'll need to learn a new skill – it's called palming.

1 First, you need to learn to palm the sponge balls – at least they aren't very large! Place one ball in the palm of your  hand. Bring your thumb over a little way to hold it in position; it shouldn't move, even when you hold your hand upright. Practise until you can keep the sponge ball in place when you are moving your hands around a lot. Now try to palm two balls!

2 Once you are really good at palming,
   you're ready to move on to the next step,
   which is tricking an audience.

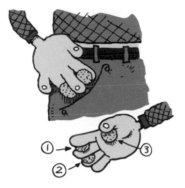

3 Have all three balls in your pocket before
   you begin your performance. Tell the
   audience you are getting two balls out of
   your pocket. Show the audience the two
   balls in your right hand. You have also
   palmed a ball, so there are really three balls
   in your right hand, but the audience must
   see only two of them.

4 Tell the audience you
   are moving one ball to
   your left hand. While
   you move the ball,
   secretly move the third
   ball to your left hand,
   too.

5 Now hold two balls up in the air, one in
   each hand, and ask your audience to agree
   that you have one ball in each hand. They,
   of course, will agree, and then you pass
   the ball from your right hand to your left
   hand, saying as you do: 'Of course, now I
   have two balls in my left hand, don't I?'

6 But, of course,
   you don't –
   there are three balls
   nestling in your hand.

7   Palming will come in very
handy throughout your
magic career – learn to do
it well!

Did you know?

During the Second World War, many magicians entertained the
troops. Magicians travelled overseas as well as performing on
home ground.

Cups and Balls

This may be the oldest magic trick – hiding a ball under a cup! Magicians all over the world learn it to entertain and confuse their audiences.

The special cups used in this trick can be purchased wherever magic props are sold; consider buying a set of clear plastic cups to begin with, so you can see exactly where each ball is as you learn. Each cup has a rim that prevents another cup from being pushed completely inside it, enabling a ball to be hidden in the space created. Also, the bottom of each cup has an indentation that,

when the cup is upside down, lets a soft
sponge ball rest on it without rolling.

1 To prepare, place the large ball in your
left pocket, one small ball in each of the
three cups and the fourth small ball in your
left hand. Place the cups inside each other.
They should be sitting mouth up.

2 When you begin the
performance, turn
each cup over quickly,
keeping the ball hidden
underneath.

3   Tap or wave your hand over all the cups and then lift the right one with your right hand to reveal a ball resting on the table underneath it. Transfer the cup to your left hand, so it covers the small ball hidden there.

4   Repeat with the other two cups, showing the two other balls and placing the cups over the one already in your left hand.

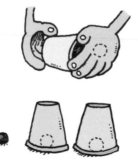

5   Now place each cup mouth down directly behind a ball on the table. Place the last cup you lifted behind the right ball. Place

the second cup you lifted behind the left
ball. Place the first cup you lifted behind
the centre ball. As you place this cup on the
table, make sure the concealed ball drops
into it before you turn it mouth down.

6   Pick up the centre ball and place it on top
of the centre cup. Next, place both the other
cups on top of the ball. With a tap or wave of
your hand, lift all three cups as one to reveal
a ball on the table. To the
audience it appears as though
you have magically made
the ball pass through the
base of the cup. Wait for the
applause . . . and then say:
'But wait, there's more!'

131

7   Hold the stack of cups mouth up so
    the hidden ball is now resting inside the
    middle cup. Separate the cups again and
    place the empty ones mouth down on the
    table, behind the right and left balls. Put
    the cup with the ball mouth down over the
    centre ball. Place a ball on top of this cup
    and repeat step 6, inviting a volunteer to
    tap the cup. While your volunteer is doing
    this, take the large ball from your pocket
    and hold it in your left hand.

8   When you lift the stack of cups again,
    astonishingly, three small balls are on the
    table. Casually place the cups mouth down
    in your left hand and
    act as though the trick
    is finished by placing
    the stack of cups
    mouth down on the
    table.

9 A bit of acting here will earn you enormous applause, so hesitate as if you want to tell your audience something, but shouldn't. Then say you'll reveal a magic secret: You did use more than three balls for the trick! Pick up the cups to reveal a much larger ball – to more applause!

Masterly Mental
Magic

A magician can gain much by learning a few
mentally challenging tricks. They always work and
they always make the magician look, well, magical!
Many are card tricks and many need a little bit of
preparation, and, of course, they all need practice
– but it's worth the trouble, as they are all terrific
tricks to perform.

Clever Colours

★ You need: six index cards.
a black marker. a table

Keeping the audience's attention on the great names of colours you have chosen will distract them from the simplicity of this trick!

1 A little preparation is necessary for this trick. Write the name of a different colour on each index card. Be creative with the names of the colours because you need a different number of letters for each colour. Perhaps you'll choose red (3), blue (4), green (5), yellow (6), magenta (7) and lavender (8).

2 Now you're ready for your audience. Place the cards randomly on a table with the names of the colours facing up and ask a volunteer to pick a colour.

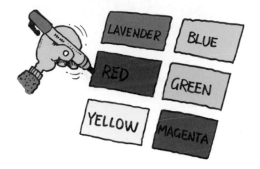

3   Your volunteer is not to tell anyone the name of the colour, but must silently spell the name of the colour, one letter at a time, as you touch each card. When your volunteer reaches the last letter of the colour, he must say 'Stop', and your hand will be resting on the correct card!

4   How does it work? Well, for the first two letters you touch any cards you want; then you touch the three-letter colour, the four-letter colour, and so on. You will always be on the correct card when the volunteer tells you to stop!

Wacky Clock

Find a really great clock face to photocopy, because the more zany it is, the more it will distract your audience from the simple, but clever, trick you are about to do for them.

1 Ask a volunteer to look at the photocopied clock face and select a number from it – silently! Ask your volunteer to

add 1 to the number she selects; so if she chooses 7, she adds 1 to make 8, keeping this all in her head.

2 If she needs to write down the number she first thought of, let her do so, but make sure you can't see it.

3 Now for the clever bit! Ask your volunteer to begin counting silently from the number she now has (in our example, the volunteer starts with 9) each time you tap your pencil on the clock's face.

4 When she gets to 20, she is to say 'Stop!' Remarkably, you will be on the correct number, so you circle it on the clock's face and hand it to your volunteer face down. She is to tell the audience the number she originally selected and then turn over the

COUNTERCLOCKWISE FROM 6

photocopy to reveal your answer. Your answer will be correct every time!

5 The secret? You begin tapping on the clock's face at the number 6 each time you do the trick and you tap counterclockwise on the numbers. When your volunteer says 'stop' at 20, you will always be on the correct number.

6 If you are going to repeat this trick in front of the same audience, make sure no one sees where you begin tapping each time.

They Match!

★ You need: two pieces of
paper, two pencils

This little trick won't fool your audience
for long, but it's great for a laugh. You tell
the audience that your powers of mental
concentration are so good that you will be
able to write the same sentence as someone
from the audience.

1 Ask a volunteer to write a sentence
on one of the pieces of paper – it can
be anything your volunteer likes. Your
volunteer then folds the paper and hands it
to another member of the audience.

2 Put the other piece of paper in front of
you and tell the audience you are going
to write the same sentence. Pretend to be
concentrating hard. Write 'You're right,

141

they match!' on your piece of paper. Fold it and hand it to the same person who is holding the sentence written by the volunteer.

3 Ask this person to open the volunteer's piece of paper and read the sentence aloud.

4 Now ask this person to open the paper containing the sentence you wrote and read it aloud. The reader will laugh (of course!) and then say, 'You're right, they match!' because that is what's written on the paper!

5   Your audience will be tremendously
    amazed and clap and cheer, until the
    reader tells them the truth!

Magic Dates

This simple but intriguing trick only requires the magician to know what year it is!

1 Write a number on one piece of paper and place it in the envelope. (Your audience will think it's a random choice, but you'll always double the current year. So if it's 2002, you'll write 4004.) Seal the envelope and ask for a volunteer.

2 When the volunteer comes forward, give him the sealed envelope and ask him to keep it in his pocket until you ask for it.

3 Give the volunteer the paper and pen and
   ask him to write down, then add up, the
   following four numbers:

   - the year he was born
   - the year he began school
   - the age he'll be at the end of this year
   - the number of years since he started
     school

4 For example, the numbers might look like
   this:

   1993
   1998
   9
   + 4
   ───
   4004

5 When the volunteer
   has finished the
   addition, ask him to
   open the envelope.
   He will be astonished

to find that you have already written the same answer and sealed it in the envelope!

6 If you want to ask an adult volunteer some questions, replace 'the year he or she began school' and 'the number of years since he or she started school' with either 'the year he or she began working' and 'the number of years since he or she began working' or 'the year he or she got married' and 'the number of years since he or she got married'. The answer will always be the same – double the current year.

Old Timers' Card Trick

★ **You need:** a deck of cards

This is a trick that works itself, so you need to keep up the entertaining patter. Practise telling your story before unleashing this on your audience.

1 Take any three cards from a full deck of cards, so you now have 49 cards in your hand.

2 Ask a member of the audience to come forward and select any card from the deck, memorise it, put it back in the deck, and then shuffle the deck thoroughly. Now, holding the cards face down, ask your volunteer to deal the cards into seven face-up overlapping rows, dealing across the rows each time.

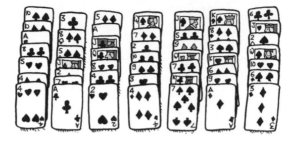

3   Stand well away as the volunteer does
this, then ask the volunteer to search
until she finds the card she memorised.
Numbering the columns from left to right,
ask her to tell you the number of the
column her card is in. Ask her to close up
the columns and stack the piles on top of
each other. She should put the second pile
on top of the first, the third on top of both,
the fourth on top again, and so on.

4   When all the piles are stacked, ask your
volunteer to turn the stack face down and
deal the cards in the same way as before.
Now request the number of the column

148

containing the selected card. Mention that you have seen magicians who ask their volunteers to repeat this part of the trick over and over, but you can see that your volunteer is tiring, so twice will be enough.

5   Ask the volunteer to pile up the cards as before (second pile upon first, third upon second, and so on), and then ask her to start dealing them out one last time. After a while, stop her and say the next card will be the one she chose. And it will be!

6   How is this so? Well, the secret is simple mathematics – there is a formula that lets you 'predict' the correct card every time! You subtract 1 from the second reported pile number and multiply this number by 7. Add on the first reported pile number, and the total gives the position of the card on the third deal.

7   So, if the card was in pile five the first
    time and pile one the second time,
    the formula would be:
    $1 - 1 = 0$; $0 \times 7 = 0$; $0 + 5 = 5$; so the fifth
    card dealt in the third round will be the
    chosen card. Often it will be a card in the
    twenties or thirties that you are waiting
    for, so it might be a good idea to practise
    looking impatient!

Linking Minds

Your audience will believe you really do have magical powers when you perform this trick.

1. All you need to do to prepare for this trick is memorise the top card in the deck.

2. Once your audience arrives, spread the deck out face down on the table. You must keep track of the top card at all times.

3   Explain that you are going to link minds with a volunteer from the audience. Ask for a volunteer to come up and stand before the table. You will call out the name of a card, and she must try to choose the card without looking at the card faces. You need to encourage her by suggesting she take her time and wait until it feels absolutely right.

4   The first card you call out is the card you memorised. Watch to see if your volunteer selects that card. The chances are very good she won't. But whatever card she selects, ask her to hand it to you without looking at it. You now look at it and say something like, 'Not bad', and put it to one side, face down, so no one can see it. The next card you call out is the card you have just seen.

5　The volunteer selects another card and hands it to you, after which you assure her she is doing well and place it face down on the table with the first card. Call out the name of the just-selected card and have the volunteer look again at the cards, select one, and hand it to you. You again reassure her she is doing well and say you'll try this time.

6　You name the last card you just looked at and say you'll concentrate on that one. You now reach over and pick up the card you memorised – which was also the first one you named. Put it with the rest and scoop up all the cards chosen.

7　For maximum effect, turn them over one by one to see how you and

your volunteer both did. Of course, every card is correct.

8 A couple of tips: If at any time your volunteer selects the card you initially memorised, end the trick there and turn over all the cards to show they are correct – don't select one yourself. Another good thing is to have another member of the audience write down the cards you call out, so you can check them later to prove they are all correct.

Riveting Rope and Ring Tricks

These tricks are good for young people to perform and for their friends to watch. Ropes and rings are easily obtainable in all lengths and colours. Specialty magic shops sell linking rings and every type of magic rope possible, so clever magicians can vary their tricks.

The Vanishing Ring

> ★ You need: a rope. a ring. a handkerchief

This is a great, simple trick to begin a routine. It looks like magic, so it must be magic!

1 First, slip the rope through the ring, just as we've shown in the illustration. Make sure the ends of the rope are knotted together so the ring appears trapped.

2 Cover the ring with the handkerchief. Ask a volunteer to hold the knotted ends of the rope while you hold the ring.

3 Now tell your audience you will need all your magical powers to free the ring without untying the rope. Tell the volunteer not to let go of the rope at any cost.

4 Deliver your patter while you keep your hands out of sight behind the handkerchief and push the rope downward over the ring.

SLIDE RING OFF ROPE

5 Utter magical words (whichever ones work best for you) as you free the ring with a flourish, ensuring the rope is still knotted and held by your volunteer. Wait for wild applause!

Two Become One

This is another trick that's easy to learn and execute. It's great to do at the start of a show.

1 You need to prepare your ropes before the audience arrives. Your aim here is for the audience to think you have two ropes of equal length knotted together. That's why the ropes must be the same colour and thickness.

2 First, tie the short piece of rope around the centre of the long piece. Don't tie it too tightly. Tie the two ends of the long

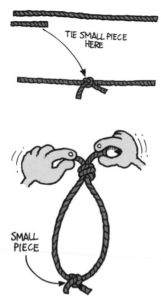

TIE SMALL PIECE HERE

SMALL PIECE

piece together as well. Does it look like you now have two pieces of rope of equal length tied together? If not, redo the knots, because that's the most important part of the trick.

3 Now for your performance. Show the ropes to the audience, holding them carefully in both hands. Tell them you are able, because of your exceptional powers, to make these two short pieces of rope into one long piece.

4   Untie the real knotted ends of the long
rope and examine it carefully, making sure
to mention the knot in the middle. Now
say you're sure you'll be able to get rid
of that pesky knot by using a few magic
words. You can even ask the audience for
their favorite magic words and use one or
more of them.

THE PESKY KNOT
(The SHORT ROPE)

5   While they are shouting out
their magic words, wind the
rope around your left hand.
Don't stop when you come to
the false knot; just hide it as
you slide it along the longer
rope into your right hand.

SLIDE KNOT
ALONG THE
LONG ROPE

6 Now utter more magic words and unwind the now completely unknotted rope from your left hand. It's now one piece!

Knots Away!

★ **You need: a length of rope**

This is a great close-up trick. You should
tell your audience you want to create
knots . . .

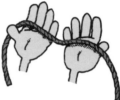

1 First, put the rope across
both hands, with your
palms up.

2 Now raise the left hand a
little, turning it so the palm
actually faces you. Do the same with the
right hand and a loop forms.

ROUND
TWICE
MORE

3 Place the loop over
your left hand and over
the end of the rope that
you are holding in your
left hand. Allow the rope to

pass under your thumb and then return the thumb to its original position.

4 Repeat the looping action twice more and put down the rope (carefully, of course!) and build up an air of expectancy with much talk about concentrating – otherwise the knots won't appear.

5 Slowly lift the rope and, as you do so – if you have performed the trick correctly – three knots will appear by magic.

Remember to speak magic words to make
the knots appear faster!

Rope Handcuffs

★ **You need: two 60 cm (24 in) lengths of cotton rope**

You'll tie your audience up in knots with this trick! (Then you'll free them, of course!)

1. Ask for two brave volunteers. Tie their wrists together with the ropes as shown in the illustration.

2. Now ask them to try really hard to release themselves from their predicament without cutting the ropes or untying the knots. Of course they won't be able to do so, and now you'll have to help them.

3. First, pull the middle of one of the ropes towards the opposite person so you create

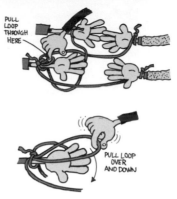

a loop. Now draw the loop to the wrist of that person and pass the loop through the rope around the wrist and pull it over the entire hand.

4 Presto! You have freed your volunteers from their rope handcuffs. Ask them to step back from each other and take the wild applause gracefully!

Just One Hand

★ You need: one length of rope measuring 90 cm (35 in)

This is another simple trick that audiences love to watch. You'll tie a knot in a rope using just one hand, and they won't know how you did it!

1 Make sure your audience sits directly in front of you. Now drape the rope across your right palm, between the thumb and index finger and behind the little finger. One end needs to be a little longer than the other (see illustration depicting A and B).

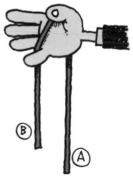

2   Give the rope an upward flick and drop
    your hand down at the same time. You
    should catch the longer end of the rope (A)
    between your index and middle fingers.

3   Now hold onto the A end of the rope
    between your index and middle fingers
    and turn your hand so your fingers are
    pointing toward the floor. The rest of the

rope will slip off your hand, forming a one-handed knot!

4 You will have to practise that upward flick – but it's worth it, as it's a classy trick when done correctly!

Did you know?

Pulling a rabbit out of a hat is supposed to be a classic trick. However, it's a trick that is rarely performed. It was probably devised by Scottish magician John Henry Anderson in the 1830s.

The Neverending Rope

⭐ You need: a piece of rope at least 90 cm (35 in) long. a table. a wand. a jacket with an inside pocket

Your friends won't mind being strung along with this clever rope trick.

1   Show your audience you are holding a short piece of rope. (In fact, you are holding the ends of your long piece of rope, but more on that later.) Explain that your powers can make the rope grow.

2 Tap the back of your hand with your wand and say some terrific magic words, and then begin to pull the rope from one end. It will continue to grow and grow and grow.

3 You can continue to pull the rope, or even better, ask a volunteer to do so for you. Once it is coiled on the table, take a bow as your audience applauds.

4 How is it done? It's simple, really. Before the show, fold the rope in half

and stuff the centre into the inside pocket.
Thread the rest of the rope up your jacket
sleeve and hold both ends in your hand.

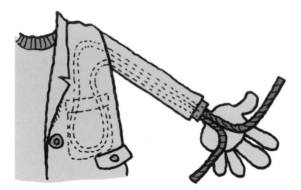

Cut and Restored Rope

★ You need: a piece of soft
rope about 1.2 m (4 ft) long,
scissors

This is a classic trick all magicians need
to perfect. You will appear to cut a piece of
rope in half, then restore it.

1　Once more, make sure your
audience is seated directly in front
of you. Drape the centre of the rope
over your index finger.

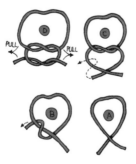

2　Bring one
end of the
rope up to the
middle and tie
a square knot.

174

3 Explain that you have magic scissors – then with a flourish, cut the rope. You must cut it in exactly the place shown in the illustration.

4 Once the cut has been made, casually put the scissors down in a place where the audience cannot see them. Now hold the rope at each end and pull it tightly so

everyone can see it's a rope with a knot in the centre.

5 Begin to wrap the rope around one of your hands – your left if you are right-handed, your right if you are left-handed. As you wrap the rope, the square knot will

175

slide off the rope and must be concealed in your free hand. While you reach for your magic scissors, quickly drop the piece of rope out of sight.

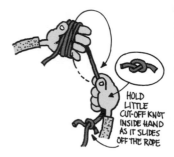

HOLD LITTLE CUT-OFF KNOT INSIDE HAND AS IT SLIDES OFF THE ROPE

6 Wave your magic scissors over your wrapped hand and recite your favourite magic words. Put down the scissors – this time in full view of your audience – unwrap the rope, and wave it about. The rope is restored!

ABRACADABRA

Fun with Magic

This is what we hope all your magic tricks will
lead to: lots of fun. There is no real theme to the
following tricks. as there has been with the ring.
rope and coin tricks. In fact. the only thing they
have in common is - yes. you've guessed
it - they're fun!

Faster than a Calculator

★ You need: a pen or pencil, a piece of paper, a calculator

Amaze your friends (and your parents!) by adding up five three-digit numbers in a few seconds, without using a calculator!

1   There is no need to prepare anything for this trick – you'll use your mental arithmetic skills!

2   Ask a volunteer to write down a three-digit number on the piece of paper. The digits must be different and cannot be consecutive, such as 1, 2, 3.

3   Ask your volunteer to repeat step 2. The
    two three-digit numbers must be different.

4   Ask for another different three-digit
    number to be written underneath the first
    two. This number is the one you are really
    concerned with – it is the key number.

5   Now you take the pen and paper
    and write a fourth number from left to
    right. Make sure the sum of the first and
    fourth numbers equals 999.

6 Write another number, making sure the sum of the second and fifth numbers equals 999.

7 Give the paper back to your volunteer and ask him to use the calculator to add the five numbers – you are not to see the total.

8 Now, when he returns the paper to you (the total is not written on it), pretend to add up the five numbers in your head within seconds. Write down the total. It will match what he has on the calculator.

(9) How? Well, remember we said the third number is the key number? It's part of a simple formula, which is:

```
2000
+ (Key number -2)
= the answer
```

(10) If your volunteer writes a 9 for the first digit anywhere, add it up to 999, but write down a two-digit number; don't bother with the 0 in front.

181

In a Tearing Hurry

This is a quick trick you can do only once for an audience – it's a great show opener or can be a bit of light relief after a long trick.

1 Before your audience arrives, make two tears in each of the two pieces of paper, creating three equal strips on each sheet. Do not tear through the sheets completely.

2 Once your audience is seated, ask for a volunteer. Hand your volunteer one of the pieces of paper. Ask her to tear away the two end pieces from the middle piece in just one tear. She won't be able to do it, but you can!

3 Pick up the other piece of paper and show her how it's done. Hold one end piece in each hand. Bend over and hold the middle piece with your lips. Now pull the outside pieces, and you will be left with three separate pieces of paper!

The Amazing Jumping Rubber Band

You only have to learn one secret move in order to perform this simple sleight of hand, but your audience will think you're an amazing magician!

1. Keeping your palm facing you, let the audience see you put a rubber band around the base of your middle and index fingers.

2. Pull the rubber band with your other hand to show that it is solid. As

you close your hand, slip all four fingertips inside it. You must do this quickly and secretly. You will need to practise getting all four fingertips into the rubber  band with a minimum of movement. When you look at your hand, you can see the rubber band stretched over the four fingers, but the audience will see it stretched around only the first two.

3   Open your hand. The band automatically (and magically!) jumps to the other two fingers.

4   Of course, now you want to make it jump back again. Put all four fingers into the band as you close your hand; then open your hand. See? The band jumps again. It works every time, once you get the hang of it!

5 If your audience is close to you and you
   want to vary the trick, use two different-
   coloured rubber bands. Put one rubber
   band around the base of the middle
   and index fingers and put the other

186

rubber band around the base of the other two fingers, then put all four fingertips into both. When you open your hand, the bands will magically swap places.

The Messy Trick

★ You need: three eggs.
three cardboard toilet paper
rolls. one broom. a pie plate.
three glasses half-full of water

In this trick, you're going to make three
eggs drop into glasses of water! You'll
probably make a mess while you are
learning this one, so don't forget to clean
up when you've finished practising!

1 Choose your location – an outside picnic
table is a good place to do this trick.

2 Allow your audience to stand around the
table, but not too near.

3 Set up the trick on the edge of the table.
The eggs should sit on top of the cardboard

rolls (make sure the eggs are the right size, if they are too small or too large to sit properly on the rolls, the trick won't work). The cardboard rolls should sit on the pie plate, and the pie plate should sit on top of the glasses (see illustration). Check that the pie plate is hanging over the edge of the table.

4 Face the table and place the broom in front of you. The bristles of the broom must be directly below the pie plate. You now step on the bristles while pulling the handle of the broom towards you.

5 As you let go, the
   handle of the broom
   will hit the pie plate
   straight on and
   things will fly!

6 The three eggs will
   fall into the half-full
   glasses of water!
   Clever magician!

Stay Awake!

You'll keep audiences awake when you show them how you change the colour of a balloon!

1 This trick requires preparation. First, insert your light-coloured balloons inside the darker ones. Now inflate each inner (light) balloon, then tie its neck with some string.

2   Now inflate each outer balloon to create an air space between the two balloons. Tie the necks of the outer balloons with the same pieces of string used to tie the inner balloons.

3   Tape a pin to the end of your wand – you want to make a bang! Prick one of the outer balloons and your audience will be amazed to see, and hear, it change colour. (If you pop both balloons at once, just tell your audience you thought they looked

sleepy and they'll miss the next wonderful trick if they doze off!)

4 Hang the balloons around the stage area so you can easily reach them during a performance. Ensure that your audience notices the balloons by referring to them: 'I'm surrounded by some fabulous purple balloons, but I do prefer yellow'.

5 If you feel the audience is not appreciative enough during any part of your show, touch one of the (outer) balloons with your wand and bang! Not only do people wake up, they realise you've changed the colour of the balloon! Pop the balloons throughout your act, ensuring no one sleeps!

No dozing in the back now. Or I may be forced to change the colour of the balloon one more time!

Ooops... I see someone dozing!

Coin of Illusion

Although you need many coins for this trick, you use none! Your audience will think you are throwing a coin from hand to hand, but it's all an illusion!

1. Make a show of taking a handful of coins from your pocket. Let the audience see the coins are real. Pretend to choose one coin and pick it up – you'll need to practise this! Return the coins to your pocket.

2. Throw the imaginary coin back and forth from one hand to the other, making a small slapping sound as you pretend to catch the coin each time. Practise with a real coin beforehand so you can get the sound right.

Slap the heel of your palm with your fingers as you 'catch' your coin, and it should sound as if you're really catching a coin.

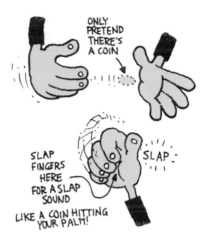

ONLY PRETEND THERE'S A COIN

SLAP FINGERS HERE FOR A SLAP SOUND LIKE A COIN HITTING YOUR PALM!

SLAP

3 Do this several times, then stop and pretend to hold the imaginary coin in one hand. Ask your audience to guess how it landed: 'Heads or tails?' Of course, upon opening your hand there is no coin. That's OK, because the audience assumes it's now in your other hand.

4 Slowly open your other hand to reveal no coin there either – and bow while your audience applauds!

Any Colour

You can choose the correct-coloured crayon every time – without looking!

1. Prepare for this trick by marking each of the crayons in a different way. You need to be able to tell which crayon is which just by feeling them. The marks, of course, cannot be obvious to anyone looking at the crayons. So, for instance, you might tear a piece of the paper from one, make a nick in the bottom of another with your fingernail or a pair of scissors,

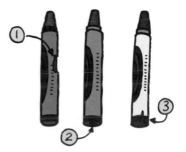

and make a nick in the top of the third one. Only you know which mark matches which colour and, naturally, you must remember this!

2 With this trick, it's important to be dramatic! You don't want your audience to notice that you are feeling for the mark on a particular crayon, so you need to distract them. Talk to your audience and explain that you're concentrating hard, trying to 'sense' the colours.

3 To perform the trick, turn away from your audience and ask a volunteer to randomly place the crayons into your hands, which you are holding behind your back.

4 Now face your
audience and ask the
volunteer to call out
one of the colours.
Start acting, while
you feel for the mark
of the particular
colour called.

5 When you find the crayon, bring it out
with a flourish and wait for the applause.
Do this trick only once or twice in a show.

Hidey Ho

★ **You need: a deck of cards, a large scarf (or hankie)**

You're such a good magician that any card you name can penetrate a solid object, such as a scarf!

1 All you have to do beforehand is secretly memorise the top card in the face-down deck and then remember not to shuffle the cards!

2 Hold the deck face up in the palm of your left hand if you're right-handed, or in your right if you are left-handed. The card you have memorised should be

MEMORISED CARD NOW ON BOTTOM OF DECK

sitting on the bottom of the deck in your palm.

3 Show the scarf to the audience – in fact, pass it around so everyone can see it's an ordinary scarf.

4 Once it's returned to you, drape the scarf over the deck of cards so its centre rests on top of the deck.

5 Make sure you draw the audience's attention to the fact you now can't see the cards. Now, reach under the scarf with your other hand and remove the deck, but leave the bottom, memorised card behind in your palm.

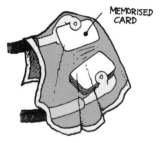

MEMORISED CARD

6 Place the deck of cards on top of the scarf, directly over the card

that is hidden under the scarf.

7   Begin to wrap the scarf around the deck of cards. Start by folding the edge nearest to you away from you with your free hand. Place the thumb of this hand underneath the memorised card and the wrapped deck. Place the rest of the fingers on top to grip the deck, and now rotate it upright so the hidden card faces you. Do this part carefully, because if you allow the hidden card to shift the audience will see it!

8   Now, keeping the hand gripping the deck where it is, use your opposite hand to fold the sides of the scarf back towards you, diagonally over the hidden card. The

folds need to overlap this card, while your thumb holds everything in place.

9 It's time to dazzle your audience! With the fist of the hand that folded the scarf, grip all the scarf hanging below and rotate the deck (keeping the hidden card facing you) so it is hanging down. If the folds are tight enough, the hidden card should stay in place when you lift your thumb.

10 Tell your audience that you can magically make any card you call appear through the scarf. Now, of course, you call the card you have memorised – the hidden card – and then shake the deck,

while chanting magic words. The hidden card will magically begin to appear as if it is penetrating the centre of the scarf. When it hits the table, allow the wrapped deck to be examined as you bask in your audience's admiration!

Counting Cards

★ You need: a deck of cards

This is a simple 'find the card' trick that works on its own, but you can make it yours with some cleverly planned patter.

1. Count out the top 10 cards from a deck of cards, but don't let your audience guess that you are counting. Use some patter to distract the audience while you set up the trick.

2 When you've counted out 10 cards, sweep them up and return them to the top of the deck, secretly glancing at the bottom card – let's say it's the eight of spades.

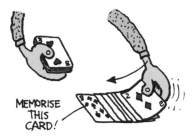

MEMORISE THIS CARD!

3 Ask the audience, or a volunteer in the audience, for a number between 10 and 19. If the number you're given is 14, for example, you count out 14 cards on the table.

4 Put the rest of the deck to one side and add the digits of the chosen number, 1 and 4, together. You get 5.

14 CARDS

5 Announce what you think the fifth card is (here, the memorised card, the eight of spades). Deal out five cards from the small pile, and the fifth card will be the eight of spades!

SMALL PILE

5th CARD will be 8 of SPADES

A No-card Card Trick

★ You need: nothing but your mind and some good patter

Finally, here's a card trick you can perform when you don't have a deck of cards handy.

1 Ask a volunteer to name a number between one and ten, then tell him he should change his mind and choose another number! He mustn't tell anyone the second number, but ask him to double it.

2 Now, ask him to add 14 to it; then divide by 2; then subtract the original number. The answer is the value of his imaginary card. He must remember it.

3 For example:

First choice	3
Second number	4
Double it	8
Add 14	22
Divide by 2	11
Subtract original (– 4)	7

4 Now ask him to concentrate on a suit of cards – either hearts, clubs, diamonds or spades. You pretend to concentrate and then blurt out a suit, for instance, 'Diamonds'.

5   It is unlikely your first guess will be right, so keep guessing until you name the right suit.

6   Of course, the audience now thinks you're having trouble with the trick, as you probably took a few guesses to get the right suit. But as soon as you guess the suit, you say something like: 'Boy, I can't believe you chose the seven of hearts [or whatever]'.

7   Pause here – you need your volunteer to realise you have chosen the correct value of the card. Then he can tell the audience how clever you are.

8   This is really a simple trick. If you ask your volunteer to add 14, the final number will be 7; if you ask him to add 10, the final number will be 5; and so on. The answer is always going to be half of the number you ask him to add.

How Many Pieces?

⭐ You need: two strips of paper about 50 cm (20 in.) by 10 cm (4 in.). a black marker. glue

This is a classic destroy-and-restore trick!

1 Before your audience arrives, write the words 'ONE PIECE' on each of the two strips of paper. Make the letters look exactly the same on both strips.

2 Fold one strip in half, then in half again, and again – until the paper only measures around 5 cm (2 in.) long and 7.5 cm (3 in.) wide.

3   Glue this tightly folded square to the back of the other strip of paper. Glue it near the end of the strip behind the word 'ONE'.

4   Now you are ready for an audience. Hold your strip of paper by the ends so the audience sees the words 'ONE PIECE'. Tell your audience you have just the one piece of paper.

5   Now tear the strip of paper in half. You must be careful not to expose the paper glued on the back. Place the torn-off strip in front of the piece with 'ONE' on it and hold them at their smooth ends.

6   Say you'd like it smaller, so tear both pieces of paper in half again, putting the pieces of the word 'PIECE' in front of the others again. Tear them one last time – by now making lots of fun of the words 'ONE PIECE'. You should now have eight pieces.

7   Fold the pieces, keeping the edges away from you and even with the secret folded piece of paper. Are you holding a packet of folded paper between your fingers and thumb of your right hand? You should be. The audience only sees torn pieces of paper but you can see one whole strip.

8   Look confused, and say something like: 'But now I've done this, I really think I prefer it as one piece.' As you say this, pass the folded packet over to your left hand and turn it around. The strip which is still in one piece should now be facing the audience.

9   Once your fingers and thumb have secured the packet,wave your hand over it and chant a few magic words. Now, dramatically open the strip so the audience can see the words 'ONE PIECE', apparently whole again!

10 The torn pieces are folded together so they shouldn't separate and fall to the floor. If they do, keep practising!

A

C

J

K

L

M

N

O

P

R

W

Y